Slim Goodbody's

GOOD HEALTH GUIDES

EXERCISING

By Slim Goodbody

Photos by Chris Pinchbeck
Illustrations by Ben McGinnis

Consultant: Marlene Melzer-Lange, M.D.
Pediatric Emergency Medicine
Medical College of Wisconsin
Milwaukee, Wisconsin

GARETH**STEVENS**
GS
PUBLISHING
A Member of the WRC Media Family of Companies

Please visit our web site at: www.garethstevens.com
For a free color catalog describing Gareth Stevens Publishing's
list of high-quality books and multimedia programs, call
1-800-542-2595 (USA) or 1-800-387-3178 (Canada).
Gareth Stevens Publishing's fax: (414) 332-3567.

Library of Congress Cataloging-in-Publication Data available upon request from publisher.
Fax (414) 336-0157 for the attention of the Publishing Records Department.

ISBN-13: 978-0-8368-7741-0 (lib. bdg.)

This edition first published in 2007 by
Gareth Stevens Publishing
A Member of the WRC Media Family of Companies
330 West Olive Street, Suite 100
Milwaukee, WI 53212 USA

Photos: Chris Pinchbeck, Pinchbeck Photography
Illustrations: Ben McGinnis, Adventure Advertising

Managing editor: Valerie J. Weber
Art direction and design: Tammy West

Printed in Canada

1 2 3 4 5 6 7 8 9 10 10 09 08 07 06

TABLE OF CONTENTS

Cavemen Did Not Drive 4

Times Change! 6

Exercise Is Fun! 8

Mighty Movers 10

Teamwork! 12

Stretch! 14

Wild Fun 16

Mighty Strong 18

More Wild Fun! 20

Happy Heart 22

Heart Helper 24

Work It Out 26

Off Your Seat! 28

Glossary 30

For More Information 31

Index 32

Words that appear in the glossary are printed in **boldface**
type the first time they occur in the text.

Cavemen Did Not Drive

In **caveman** times,
Life was rougher.
To **survive**,
Folks were tougher.
Up and moving on their feet
Searching for some food to eat
Or running fast and being chased
By **saber-tooths** who liked their taste.
If they wanted to escape,
They had to be in tip-top shape

4

Our **ancestors** had to work hard to find food and avoid danger. They did not have machines to help them get things done. They had to depend on their own muscle power.

If they wanted to visit friends in faraway caves, they had to walk.

If they were cold, they had to carry heavy logs out of the forest to make a fire.

If they were hungry, they had to go out and hunt for food.

Cavemen needed to be fit to stay alive.

Long after the time of cavemen, exercise stayed a normal part of life. For thousands of years, people like the Egyptians, Incas, Vikings, Romans, and Native Americans led very active lives. All around the world, people were on the go. The human body was used to being active.

Something to Think About

The ancient Greeks held the first **Olympic Games** over twenty-five hundred years ago. These games honored strength and fitness.

Times Change!

Today, life is a lot different. We have invented all kinds of machines and tools to help us get things done.

If we want to talk with friends in the next town, we call them on the telephone.

If we are cold, we flip a switch to turn on the furnace. If we are hungry, our parents drive a car to the supermarket.

All of this makes life easier. However, easier does not mean healthier. Today, most people spend too much time sitting down and too little time in motion.

All of this sitting is not good for us. Our bodies are built for action. Without enough exercise, we cannot stay healthy.

Time Spent
Sitting Everday

In car or school bus:
45 minutes

At desk in school:
5 hours

Watching television:
2 hours

Working on computer:
45 minutes

Total: 8 $\frac{1}{2}$ hours

Something to Think About

How much time do you spend sitting down?
Add up all the time you spend sitting in the car or
school bus. Add on your time at your school desk,
watching television, or working on the computer.

Exercise Is Fun!

Exercise is important for everybody. It does not matter if you are young or old, big or little, or a boy or a girl. If you want to be healthy, you need to exercise.

Exercise helps make your heart, your lungs, your bones, and your muscles stronger. It gives you energy to stay **alert** through the day. It helps you feel better, look better, and sleep better.

There are so many fun ways to get the exercise you need. You can run, skip, hop, or jump rope. You can swim, ski, dance, or go for a hike. You can kick a ball, fly a kite, or ride your bike.

You can exercise inside or outside, alone or with friends, play sports or tag.

Something to Think About

You have 1 heart, 2 lungs, 206 bones, and more than 600 muscles. You also have about 60,000 miles (96,540 kilometers) of **blood vessels.** All of these body parts need exercise to stay healthy.

Mighty Movers

The job of those six hundred mighty muscles is to move you around. Without muscles, you would be stiff as a stick and still as a statue.

You could not slide, bend, reach, twist, lift, flip, or walk.

Sternocleidomastoids: Move head

Intercostals (between ribs): Move ribs and help you breathe and turn the upper half of the body

Sartorii: The longest leg muscles, which assist in turning the legs out

Pectorals: Bend upper arm across the chest

Biceps: Bends the elbow

Abdominals: Lift upper chest

Quadriceps: Straighten the leg

If you want your muscles to work well, you need to exercise. Exercise makes muscles **flexible** and strong.

FLEXIBLE
muscles let you bend, stretch, twist, and move freely.

STRONG muscles
let you lift, carry, push, and pull heavy things.

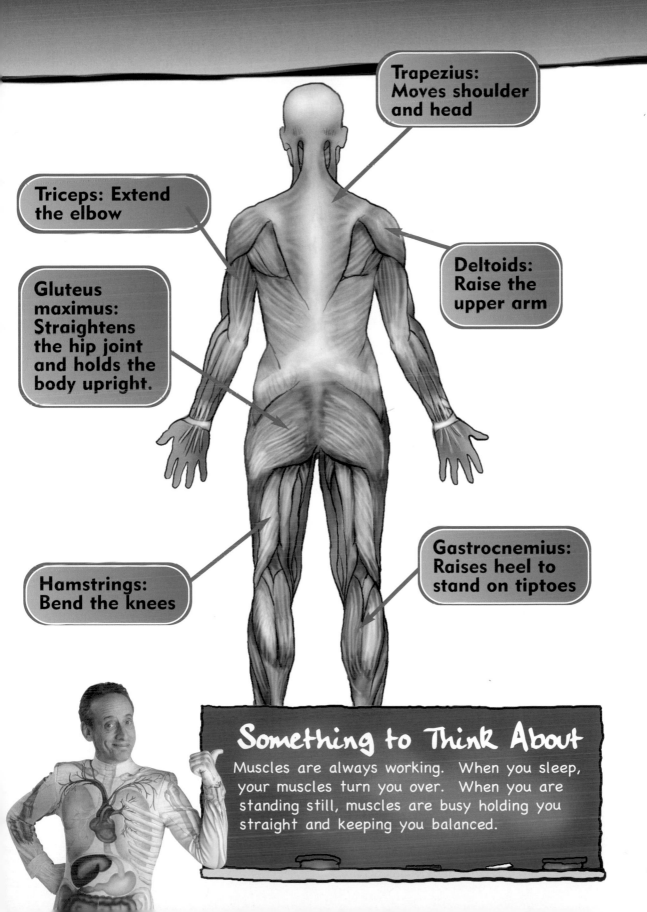

Trapezius: Moves shoulder and head

Triceps: Extend the elbow

Deltoids: Raise the upper arm

Gluteus maximus: Straightens the hip joint and holds the body upright.

Hamstrings: Bend the knees

Gastrocnemius: Raises heel to stand on tiptoes

Something to Think About

Muscles are always working. When you sleep, your muscles turn you over. When you are standing still, muscles are busy holding you straight and keeping you balanced.

Teamwork!

Muscles do not work alone. They team up with bones.

You have 206 bones in all. These bones meet at **joints**. When muscles pull on bones, the bones move at the joints.

Different joints let your body move in different ways.

Elbow joints let your arms bend.

Joints in your spine let you bend over.

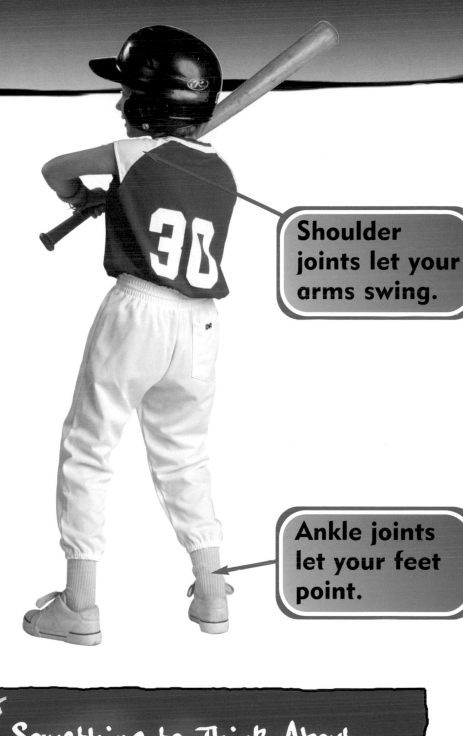

Shoulder joints let your arms swing.

Ankle joints let your feet point.

Something to Think About

If you had no joints in your legs, you could not kick a ball. You could not even sit down in a chair. If you had no joints in your arms, could you eat? Could you comb your hair?

Stretch!

If someone is flexible, it means that their muscles and bones can move freely without feeling tight or stiff. Try this experiment and see how flexible you are:

Stand with your legs straight and knees bent a tiny bit. Bend forward and try to touch the floor. If you can only reach your knees, your muscles are tight. If you can touch your toes, your muscles are flexible. If you can reach farther and touch the floor with your fingertips, you are more flexible. If you can place your palms flat on the floor, you are super flexible!

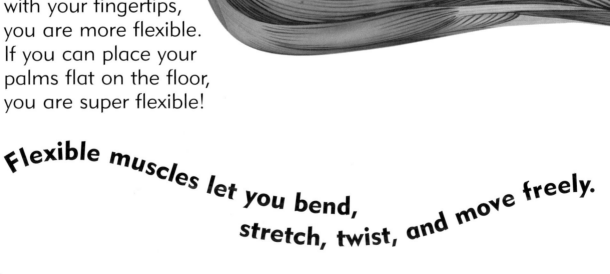

Flexible muscles let you bend, stretch, twist, and move freely.

Stretching exercises help you become more flexible. On the next page, you will find six stretching exercises that you can try.

Here are tips for doing them safely:

1 Never stretch a cold muscle. Jog in place a couple of minutes before starting.

2 Make sure to do the exercises slowly.

3 Keep breathing. Do not hold your breath while stretching.

4 Hold each stretch for 3 to 5 seconds.

5 Stretch until you can feel the muscle working.

6 Do not stretch to the point of pain.

7 If you feel pain, stop.

8 Never bounce while stretching.

9 Try to stretch a little bit more each day but not too much!

10 After doing these exercises for awhile, you can hold the stretch longer. Work up to holding stretches for 10 seconds.

Something to Think About

Different muscles move different joints. You can be flexible in some parts of your body but not in others. You may have been able to touch your toes but not clasp your hands behind your back like this. ➞

Wild Fun

Animals have a lot to teach us about being flexible. Try doing these stretches, which are based on the way animals move. Do each of these exercises about five times. Whenever the exercise says "hold," do it for 5 seconds.

Owl **Stretch:**

This stretch is good for flexible neck muscles.

1. Begin with your feet together, hands by your side, and your head level.

2. Gently turn your head as far as you can and look over your right shoulder.

3. Return to starting position.

4. Repeat this stretch on the other side, looking over your left shoulder.

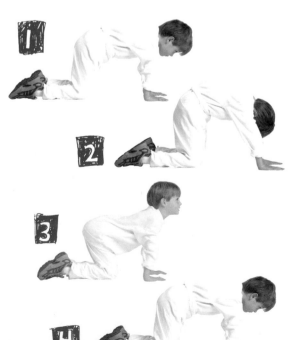

Cat **Stretch:**

This stretch is good for a flexible spine.

1. Begin on all fours with your back level. Keep your hands flat and your knees under your hips. Look straight down.

2. Arch your back as high as you can. Bring your chin to your chest and hold the position for 10 seconds.

3. Drop your stomach down toward the floor and look up to the sky. Take a nice big breath.

4. Return to starting position.

Down Dog:

This stretch is good for your whole body.

1. Begin on all fours with your back level. Keep your hands flat and your knees under your hips. Look straight down.

2. Straighten your legs as you press your heels down toward the floor.

3. Straighten your arms all the way and gently swing your head in through your shoulders.

4. Return to starting position.

Flamingo Stretch:

This stretch is good for your legs and arms.

1. Stand straight with your feet together and hands at your sides.

2. Bend your left knee and grab hold of your ankle with your left hand. Bend your right knee slightly and lift your right arm. Point your fingers upward.

3. Return to starting position.

4. Repeat the stretch on the other side.

Something to Think About

Some other exercises that help flexibility are tumbling, diving, and dancing.

Mighty Strong

Flexibility is important, but you also need to do exercises that make your muscles strong.

Strong muscles help you run faster,
jump higher, swim farther,
and hike longer.
Strong muscles help you climb trees,
skip rope, dance, and play sports.

Strong muscles help you have fun without getting tired out!

There are really two kinds of muscle strength:

1 The strength to lift a really heavy weight once. (Imagine a big pile of books so heavy that you have to use all your might to lift it one time.)

2 The strength to lift a lighter weight over and over. (Imagine you had to move those books to another classroom. You would lift fewer books but make more trips.)

It is not healthy for children to lift very heavy weights. Your muscles are still growing, and you can strain them too much. It is much better to lift a lighter weight and do it over and over again.

Something to Think About

To get stronger, muscles must be worked harder than usual. When you do the exercises on the next page, push yourself a little. Listen to your body, though, and stop if you feel any pain.

More Wild Fun!

Wild animals need to stay active to survive. All their exercising makes them stronger. Here are some animal moves that you can borrow. They will help you get stronger, too!

Butterfly Wings:

This exercise is good for your stomach muscles.

1. Lie on your back. Keep your knees bent, your feet flat, and your arms out to the sides.

2. Bring your arms and knees up toward ceiling.

3. Straighten your arms and legs and clasp your hands together.

4. Return to starting position.

Crab Walk:

This exercise is good for your arm and leg muscles.

1. Place your hands and feet flat on the floor with your fingers pointing toward your feet. Lift your back off the floor.

2. Step forward with your right arm and left leg.

3. Next, step forward with left arm and right leg.

4. Crab walk across the floor.

Duck Walk:

This exercise is good for your leg and back muscles.

1. Stand with your legs a little bit apart. Keep your knees bent, your elbows out, and your hands on your hips. Look forward.

2. Take a step with your left leg, keeping your knees bent. Lean forward a little more to keep your back flat.

3. Step forward with your right leg.

4. Duck walk across the room.

Rising Frog:

This exercise is good for your leg and arm muscles.

1. Stand with your legs apart. Your feet should be directly in line with your shoulders. Bend your knees as if you were sitting in a chair. Keep your elbows bent, your arms by your side, and your fingers spread wide.

2. Straighten your legs.

3. Reach your arms outward and upward as high as you can.

4. Return to starting position.

Something to Think About

The next time you are at the zoo, take a good look at the lions, apes, and other animals. See how strong their muscles look. Now imagine how much stronger they would be if they lived out in the wild!

Happy Heart

Your heart is a very special muscle, but it does not move any bones. Your heart's job is to pump blood. The blood brings food and oxygen to every one of your **cells**. Moving that blood is a big job because you have trillions of cells that are working all the time. To get all these cells what they need, your heart must beat about eighty times every minute. It even beats when you are asleep.

Day after day, week after week, month after month,

$1 \times 60 = 60$

$60 \times 24 = 1,440$

$1,440 \times 7 = 10,080$

$10,080 \times 62 = 524,160$

and year after year, it keeps going. Your heart is the hardest working muscle in your body!

Its scientific name is the **cardiac** muscle.

Try this experiment:

Open and close your hand eighty times quickly. Does it make your hand muscles tired? Can you imagine doing this every minute of every day? Your heart does it.

Something to Think About

When your heart gets stronger, it pumps more blood with each beat. It does not have to beat as many times each minute to do its job. This gives it a chance to rest a little, which keeps it healthier. If your heart beats even one less time each minute, it really adds up.

One less heartbeat a minute equals
60 fewer heartbeats an hour.
60 fewer heartbeats an hour equals
1,440 fewer heartbeats a day.
1,440 fewer heartbeats a day equals
10,080 fewer heartbeats a week.
10,080 fewer heart beats a week equals
524,160 fewer heart beats a year.
524,160 is more than 1/2 million.

Exercise can save your heart more than one-half million beats each year!

Heart Helper

If you want a strong and healthy heart, you need to do the right kind of exercises. You must do them five days a week. These exercises:

1 **get your heart beating faster**
2 **last for 30 minutes or more without stopping.**

Here is a list of heart helpers that will do the trick: Jogging, biking, swimming, jumping rope, hiking, cross-country skiing, dancing, in-line skating, and brisk walking.

When you do these exercises, you want your heart to work hard but not too hard. You need to push yourself a little, but do not overdo it.

Here is a simple test to let you know if you are doing too much:

If you are exercising and cannot talk easily because you are out of breath, you are working too hard.

If you exercise with energy, then day by day, your heart will grow stronger. These exercises also help your breathing muscles become more powerful. They will make you breathe deeper.

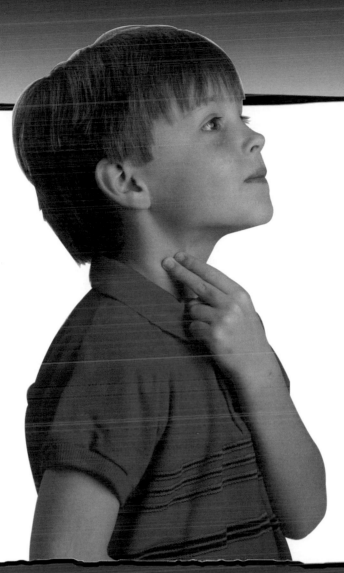

Something to Think About

A better way to know how hard your heart is working is to take your own **pulse.** You need to do this after you have been exercising for about 5 minutes. Here is how:

Place your index and middle finger on one side of your neck right under the jawbone. Press in slowly until you feel your pulse beating. It is important that you press very gently. Once you feel the pulse, stop exercising while you count how many times it beats in 10 seconds. If your heart beats between twenty-five and thirty times in 10 seconds, you are doing a great job. If it is beating faster, slow down a bit. If it is beating slower, push your pace.

Move your fingers away and start exercising again. You should check your pulse again after 20 minutes or so of exercising.

Work It Out

You have learned many kinds of exercises. Now it is time to put them together in a workout. A workout is like a journey. It has a beginning, middle, and end.

The Beginning of the Journey

To get your muscles ready for action, begin with a warm-up. A warm-up has two parts.

Part 1: Walk in place slowly with your hands at your sides. After a minute, walk faster. After another minute, lift your knees higher and swing your arms. Finally, jog in place for 2 minutes. Do not work too hard — just get your heart beating a little faster.

Part 2: Stretch for 5 to 10 minutes. Be sure to work the muscles in different parts of your body.

The Middle of the Journey

This is the longest and most active section. The middle has two parts:

Part 1: Do five or six exercises to make your muscles stronger. Be sure to work the muscles in different parts of your body.

Part 2: Do 30 minutes of a heart-helper exercise.

26

The End of the Journey

Now you need to give your heart a chance to slow down and your muscles a chance to cool down. The end has two parts:

Part 1: Walk in place for a few minutes until your heartbeat slows down. Take deep, slow breaths.

Part 2: Do 5 more minutes of stretching exercises.

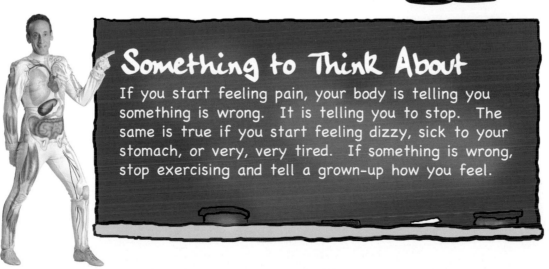

Something to Think About

If you start feeling pain, your body is telling you something is wrong. It is telling you to stop. The same is true if you start feeling dizzy, sick to your stomach, or very, very tired. If something is wrong, stop exercising and tell a grown-up how you feel.

Off Your Seat!

If cavemen came here from the past,
Imagine their surprise
At how much time we sit around
And do not exercise.

It may be fine to sit a bit,
But not the whole day long.
So do your part to make your heart
And other muscles strong.

GONE
EXERCISING

Your body loves to move, and your muscles need lots of exercise to stay healthy. Every day, look for chances to be active. Ride your bike, play tag, run with friends in the park or playground, or go for a walk with your parents. Even if you are watching television, you can get down on the floor and do some push-ups or sit-ups.

Your body will say,
"Thanks for keeping me healthy!"

Something to Think About

Your parents and other grown-ups can help you do many things, but no one can exercise for you. If you are not used to being active, do not start off doing too much. Take time to build up. Do a little more each day. You will be glad you did.

Glossary

alert — watchful and ready to act quickly

ancestors — people from whom an individual or group is descended

blood vessels — the tubes through which blood flows in the body

cardiac — relating to the heart

caveman — describing a person living in a cave long, long ago during the Stone Age

cells — tiny units that are the basic building blocks of living things

flexible — able to bend and stretch easily

joints — places where two or more bones come together in the body

Olympic Games — a festival started in Greece in 776 B.C. in which athletes compete in many different sports events

pulse — a regular beat caused by arteries stretching as the heart pumps blood

saber-tooths — short for *saber-toothed tigers*, large animals from the cat family with long, sharp teeth; saber-toothed tigers died out long ago

survive — to stay alive

For More Information

BOOKS

The Busy Body Book: A Kid's Guide to Fitness. Lizzy Rockwell (Crown Books for Young Readers)

My Amazing Body: A First Look at Health and Fitness. Pat Thomas (Barron's Educational Series)

Physical Fitness. My Health (series). Alvin Silverstein, Virginia B. Silverstein, and Laura Silverstein Nunn (Franklin Watts)

Who Am I?: Yoga for Children of All Ages. Jane Lee Wiesner (Warwick Publishing)

WEB SITES

BAM! Body and Mind
www.bam.gov/sub_physicalactivity/index.html
This site from the Centers for Disease Control and Prevention helps you plan your exercise activities, challenges your knowledge about exercise, and teaches you more about great ways to stay in shape.

Healthy Hopping
www.urbanext.uiuc.edu/hopping/index.html
Find fun ways to be more active through jumping rope and learn how to have more nutritious meals and snacks.

Slim Goodbody
www.slimgoodbody.com
Discover loads of fun and free downloads for kids and parents.

Note to educators and parents: The publisher has carefully reviewed these Web sites to ensure that they are suitable for children. Many Web sites change frequently, however, and Gareth Stevens, Inc., cannot guarantee that a site's future contents will continue to meet our high standards of quality and educational value. Be advised that children should be closely supervised whenever they access the Internet.

Index

animal exercises 16–17, 20–21
  butterfly wings 20
  cat stretch 16
  crab walk 20
  down dog 17
  duck walk 21
  flamingo stretch: 17
  owl stretch 16
  rising frog 21

biking 9, 24, 29
bones 8, 9, 12, 14, 22

dancing 9, 17, 18, 24

flexiblity 10, 14, 15, 16, 17, 18,

healthy heart 24
heartbeat 23, 27
hiking 9, 18, 24

jogging 9, 24
joints 12, 13, 15
jumping rope 9, 24

lifting 10, 17, 19, 20, 26

muscles 5, 8, 9, 10, 11, 12, 14, 15, 16, 18, 19, 20, 21, 22, 23, 24, 26, 27, 28, 29

Olympic Games 5

pain 15, 19, 27
pulse 25

skating 24
skiing 9, 24
strength 5, 8, 10, 18, 19, 20, 21, 23, 24, 26, 28
stretching 10, 14, 15, 16, 17, 26, 27
swimming 9, 18, 24

walking 24
workout 26

About the Author

John Burstein (also known as Slim Goodbody) has been entertaining and educating children for over thirty years. His programs have been broadcast on CBS, PBS, Nickelodeon, USA, and Discovery. Over the years, he has developed programs with the American Association for Health Education, the American Academy of Pediatrics, the National YMCA, the President's Council on Physical Fitness and Sports, the International Reading Association, and the National Council of Teachers of Mathematics. He has won numerous awards including the Parent's Choice Award and the President's Council's Fitness Leader Award. Currently, Mr. Burstein tours the country with his multimedia live show "Bodyology." For more information, please visit slimgoodbody.com.